a love letter
to those who
left me behind

a love letter to those who left me behind

a poetry collection by
RACHEL LABERGE

table of contents

This is for the people who loved me enough to stick around…

And for the ones who didn't.

hear me out...

love letters are never written
in a single night
but over a span of time when your
soul knows it's right

this letter is slow to start
but gets clearer with each page
words for those who left me
some during my most vulnerable stage

i promise, this is a love letter
even for those who didn't care
to love me like i loved them
never their main, mostly a spare

love takes time to grow
in ways we don't think
this is a love letter to those
who helped me bloom
and those who made me shrink

Rachel LaBerge

a love letter to those who left me behind

part one

who are you?

nostalgia

some of my earliest memories
still make me feel like an underdog
trying anything
everything
all i wanted was
to be seen
have a chance

from bus stops
to lunch rooms
and every recess in between

do you see me?

a love letter to those who left me behind

imperfections & reflections

i hate mirrors
my reflection taunts
everything on repeat
the reminder haunts
find a way to fit
can you be less?
your edges are wrong
less is best
i look at the floor
when i walk by
the mirror, another enemy
no matter how hard i try

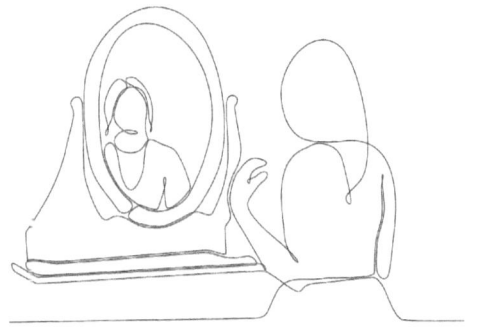

listen up, class

i'm learning
the ropes
how do i juggle
make the space
for
discovery
clipping the corners
grasping
all while trying
to be cautious
and aware of
potential snags

a love letter to those who left me behind

should i run?

my steps grew quiet
dainty and light
i'd rather be invisible
than caught in a fight
tip toe, step by step
strategically placed
are the mines
if i was careful enough
maybe i'd see the signs
take cover before
the blast and debris

what i learned first
           was how to flee

endless questions

am i enough?
all the while
not trying too hard
to be the things they crave
and i desperately hope for

am i enough?
        oh no.

a love letter to those who left me behind

show me your cool girl mask

i spend my time
trying to perfect
the mask

you know the one

the one
that
conceals
  self manipulates
      blends in
    dulls
 dims
fits

matches the uniform
proves i can keep
it all below the surface

bit by bit

stupidly easy to lose
when you're putting on a show
slight adjustments, almost trivial
who will even know?
aim for their expectations
neatly wrapped
    tied with a bow
but when you pause
    just for a minute

you're entirely
someone
different

a love letter to those who left me behind

hearts and spades

dig
until your hands are blistered
and your muscles ache
dig
make your mark
and dangle your worth
dig
what can you give?
dig
what will they take?
dig

hands and knees

maybe it'd be better
to be nothing
instead of what
you made me feel

a shadow
    a ghost
        whisper of a soul

you kept me crawling
back
    back
        back
like i was something to fix
and i let you

a love letter to those who left me behind

the way it escalates

at first, it's like a soft scrub
looking for a shine
and then it's a slow peel
to fit and fall in line
but the scrubs turn to grips
and the peels turn to gashes
reduced to chunks of "me"
the rest can be found in the ashes

it'd be different if you
kept what you took

shedding pieces of myself
like a snake
without question, mine to lose
and theirs to take
how much can someone
leave behind
until they're something different
abstract and undefined
a dangerous game to play
yourself as the bet
because pieces last only so long
and you're bound to forget

a love letter to those who left me behind

enough?

fickle and delicate
unclear at best
approval is the thing
rattling my chest

do i make the cut?
will the doubt ever leave?
is it enough?
will i earn reprieve?

there's no ribbon
at the end of this race
each day, interaction
struggling to make my case

putting them first

do you know what it's like
to be an afterthought
contemplate your self-worth
stomach
   in a knot
mask the disappointment
program your smile
   like a robot
when they were always top of mind
  while you clearly
    were not

a love letter to those who left me behind

you, with the barbed words

where did you learn
how to put your words
in like hooks
and pull enough to keep
my attention
my direction
with just enough tension

who taught you
how to keep someone
by almost letting them go

i'm an amateur

seems like everyone knows
what's expected

seems like everyone has been preparing
for years

seems like everyone practices on the
social balance beam
as soon as they can walk

everyone
besides me

a love letter to those who left me behind

you can't tell me anything

i contorted myself to fit
went to lengths
i'm embarrassed to admit
i poured and poured

i made it to the end
of this socially acceptable maze
i wanted a clap on the back
you promised "one of these days"

no one quite understood
how i needed someone
who took what they wanted
just to leave me for good

check the box

why does this feel
like a to-do list
endless
extensive

one that will
never be checked

your invisible ink
certainly doesn't help

a love letter to those who left me behind

the start of a love letter

little did i know
my letters would start here
driven from the need to fit
fed by crippling fear

i was all in
no matter the cost
i tried to love them
but i felt lost

this was the expectation
give enough, give even more
lose yourself, bit by bit
is this better than before?

Rachel LaBerge

a love letter to those who left me behind

part two

false victories

can't put my finger on it

a set never quite full
always itching my brain
buried in late night laughs
is a snag, some sort of strain
can't quite catch it
brevity its greatest skill
a wave of water controlled
until it's ready to spill
this is what i craved
isn't this what i wanted?
my ghosts sleep over
and i was always haunted

a love letter to those who left me behind

is there air in the middle?

it's not the top i'm after
but the middle ground
the place where smiles are easy
and the air is a bit lighter
where i can let my guard down
push the doubt
far enough to breathe in deep
rib to rib

it's not the top i'm after
but the middle ground
where i can breathe

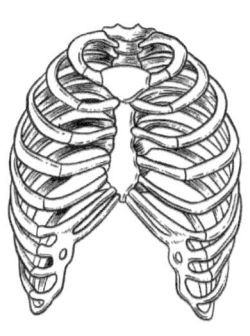

never kept

i didn't want you to make a promise
my soul begged
my heart pleaded
fear crept in and set up camp
no matter how many
times you repeated
what i meant, how i fit
the piece you were missing
now completed
i didn't want you to make a promise
it was honesty
i needed

a love letter to those who left me behind

the part that knew

our circle
connection
too good to be true
waiting for the lapse
falling
drop of the other shoe
tried to ride it out
in the moment
part of the crew
volatile
i felt the shift
bet you did too
part of your plan?
maybe not
but right on cue

referees and points

you get one
and i get zero
where do we keep the tally?

always feeling so small
if someone wants to keep score
they were never yours at all

a love letter to those who left me behind

you never meant it

you let me sink
completely, too deep
i should've stayed home
fought for sleep

instead i drove over, hopes high
the warm night buzzed
an open midnight sky

your mouth and hands screamed
"i love you"
looking back
there was no way it was true

we both were tricked
caught in your net
a memory i wish
i could forget

shallow is best

if you feel hollow
and barely an inch deep
congratulations!
you're on track

a love letter to those who left me behind

twist the plot

you've done it
captured the win
put on the cool girl costume
originality under your skin
this is your reward
fall in line
keep putting on the costume
convince yourself
everything is fine

this is what you wanted
    what you hoped for all along
but what happens when you
    wish for something desperately wrong

where'd you find this power?

how can you make me fly
    over mountains of doubt
how can a single smile
    bring water to a drought
how can the paper in my hand
    scribbled, folded, and battered
make me feel like more
    like i'm someone
    who finally mattered?

a love letter to those who left me behind

pretending you don't know

life changes and shifts
but i kept space
at times we were delicate
like the lightest of lace
if i grabbed and pulled
we'd fall apart
maybe we weren't made to last
and i knew it from the start

levels to this

sleep is no longer
out of reach
but much easier to find
gone is the exhaustion
driven by despair
and the effort of trying
tonight, in this bed
tucked in and slipping
away
i'm not dreading the sun
for what waits
the next day

a love letter to those who left me behind

take a long lock

it feels like i've ended up
where i wanted
surrounded by the people
i craved
doing what i dreamed of
grateful each day
you've stayed
as long as my brain stays busy…
it feels like a reward

hold out

i put my faith
in things i couldn't see
or trust
i held out hope
it would work out
all in or bust
i wished on stars
impatiently
for nights on end
i got a taste
of being part of it
in on the trend

a love letter to those who left me behind

blind spots

drunk
off validation
slipped notes
secrets
and inside jokes
drunk
off acceptance
phone calls
and weekend plans
drunk
off inclusion
a place to be
people to see

might need to glue it into place

my cheeks pinch
they ache
from this smile
do they know it's fake?

a love letter to those who left me behind

internal questions

i feel like i could
love you
forever
happily entangled in your web
turning a blind eye
like you want me to

i could love you forever
what does that say about me?

final placement correction

what's worse than thinking
you've won?
nabbed a place in the top ten?

how about when the prize
is companionship and inclusion
and all you want is a friend?

a love letter to those who left me behind

part three

the break

a love letter to those who left me behind

shards to reconstruct

i was made of glass
and you broke me
like you meant it
what you wanted
have you ever tried to glue something
back together?
restore what it was?

no matter what you do
how meticulous…

it's never quite the same

i really thought you'd stay

i flinch when i remember us together
the connection ran deep
we'd conquer it all, friends forever
no hill too steep
we promised to stand by
through life, changes, seasons
but then it was too hurtful to try
and i had too many reasons

a love letter to those who left me behind

coexisting

and i'll never forget when
it clicked
unsure of how monumental
it'd be

the truth clear and brutal
if i was choosing you
i'd never get the chance
to choose me

sly lies

it wasn't a promise
but a threat
you said forever
i was in your debt
cunning as a fox
a clever disguise
loneliness the barter
no match for your lies

a love letter to those who left me behind

bag of tricks

you stole pieces of me
kept them like a secret
a quiet conquest
until you had enough
to complete the puzzle
but the only thing left
was a sad, shameful shell
of the girl you used to know

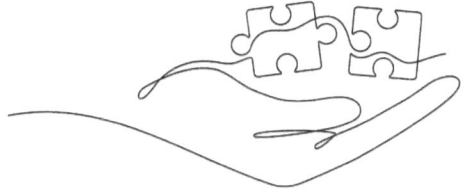

too patient, too naive

you tricked
and you took
what you wanted
without a look
back to the
one you faked out
promises and the future
you argued with doubt
i knew something
could feel it deep
in my breaths
and heartbeat
even if i knew
i tried to advance
at least wanted to
give us a chance

a love letter to those who left me behind

stripped down

my shadow
the only thing left
i willingly gave up the rest
because there was no other way
you expected it
i needed to pass the test
the edges are blurred
i can barely see it
i feel the pull in my chest
the want to mend
reassemble the pieces
who would've guessed

emergency escape plans

retreat
get out
this isn't what is seems
run
make way
nightmares instead of dreams
hide
give way
take me back to the start
hope
persevere
heal your heart

a love letter to those who left me behind

hate that you stay

you made a promise
"i'll never leave"
which you kept

but it wasn't you that remained

it was my self-doubt
aggressive and willing
to always be around

shadows and silhouettes

i'm standing
among the wreckage
pleading
how did i get here?

no ears to listen
or hands to hold
with such ease
you've unlocked my greatest fear

what if this is all for nothing
and i end up back at the start
this time all cracked and broken
who wants
someone
with a black heart?

a love letter to those who left me behind

something better

they prepare you
for love that's run its course
romantic partners leaving
finding something else

but no one tells you
about the platonic love
the one you depend on
to feel whole
up and going
pulling on lifelong strings
and taking good memories with them
leaving you with the bad

sore spots

just like shrapnel
shards and remnants piercing my skin
difficult to find
painful to remove
almost impossible to forget

you tied yourself to me
in the most agonizing of ways

a love letter to those who left me behind

torture by design

you were smart
when you left your marks
scrapes, smudges, and scars
inside, where only i can see

like a sore
   constellation
       of scars

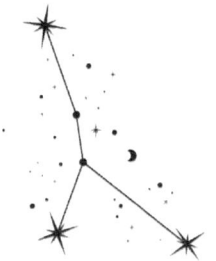

fingers crossed behind a back

you said forever
like a promise
a solemn oath
i believed we were safe
bars of time
on our side

you said forever
    but that drifted
you said forever
    but that shifted

i wanted to shake you
scream
into the void
i wanted you to mean it
you said forever

the end…
      i should've seen it

a love letter to those who left me behind

feathers and flames

for all the times i was a feather
light, carefree, vibrant
you were the flame
taking every opportunity
to singe my edges
wreck something like a game
take something whole
and ruin it to build your ego
your darkness never to tame

i was the feather
and you were the flame

2019

the things i counted on
dwindled and faded
forever turned grey
perspective is jaded
i don't have it in me
to keep running this pace
my body is exhausted
from the incessant chase
but you don't text
and i don't call
maybe you never knew me...
never knew me at all?

a love letter to those who left me behind

over-sharing

you took what you wanted
without a second guess
i gave, blindly
not wanting to be less

each time it cracked
what i needed whole
until i was taped together
losing control

one shift away from crumbling
barely there, thin and frail
you knew where to pull
where the tape would ultimately fail

wasted wishes

your intentions
were always crystal clear
no matter what
i told myself that year
this was for the corners
and obscure places
fuzzy times when
we'd blur into a sea of faces
you loved me just enough
calculated to the touch
the blind eye was a choice

i wanted us so much

a love letter to those who left me behind

the finish line i dreaded

to the one
who pulled
far enough away
that they couldn't
come back
there was no "someday"

i know it now
even if i didn't know it then
i love you
for rushing us to the end

did you keep my notes?

you tricked me
got me good
loved me in the quiet
the only way you would

you tried to walk it back
got rid of me swift and quick
like i was easy to lose
someone else the easy pick

here's to the notes we write
the pens and the paper
the ones clutched, before minds are changed
adoration and love turned to vapor

a love letter to those who left me behind

part four

what did you learn?

a love letter to those who left me behind

hands to hold

my corner of the ring used to be empty
cobwebs and dust
i can feel the absence if i try hard enough
but only because my mind trusts
that it's not reality
and it's all in the past
gone are the things
i treated like glass
my corner used to be dark
in the worst kind of way
going back is tough
but i do it to pay
my respects to what
it took to get this far
sometimes i try to
count the scars
but my corner is no longer empty
honest souls brought their light
shared it, without question
no wins to score, or preconceived spite
the darkness brought me here
to people who support with no agenda
to tie our strings, lift and pull
and be there for leaning

Rachel LaBerge

**understanding and agreeing
are two different things**

the cruelty was actually insecurity
swapped one for the other
it kept bubbling up and coming back
the only thing to do was smother
not ready for change
not ready for a hard look
at what it meant
or what you took

a love letter to those who left me behind

stand on the soles of sore feet

when do we choose ourselves
instead of waiting to be picked?
we're constantly craving selection
afraid of being missed or skipped
do whatever it takes to be considered
are we following the right script?
anything we can to be included
is it our own minds
or others we've tricked
now a hollow version
carefully calculated to depict
what we think they're looking for
take our honest qualities and constrict

prick, draw blood

quit folding your corners
rounding out the quirks
the sharpness is unique, your own
those asking for less volume
weaker opinions, a muted stance
these are people you have
clearly outgrown

a love letter to those who left me behind

falling short
and falling ahead

you deciding i wasn't enough
was one of the best things
that ever happened

no matter how much it
stung
hurt
ached

no matter the way
it crushed me

you deciding i was inadequate
was a turning point
not one i wanted
but one i desperately needed

part of my heart
is in north carolina

you matched my heart
on a monday in september
a time before you
i can barely remember
it's like a piece clicked
something i'd been trying to find
not just then but always
a soul effortlessly tied to mine

a love letter to those who left me behind

february 13, 2010

loving you
is one of my greatest
accomplishments
of this beautiful life

Rachel LaBerge

don't always get what you want

you left me behind
but i gave up the chase
you broke my heart
but i gave myself grace
you wanted me to beg
but my knees were too worn
you wanted me to wither away
but i refused to mourn

you thought i'd crawl back
but my feet
are firmly planted
you didn't think i'd do it
but it was *you*
   who took *me*
      for granted

a love letter to those who left me behind

dive in

in a sweetly chaotic moment between
words, ideas, conversation
that grin

didn't wait another second on land
made a break for the water
dove right in

your kiss taught me to swim

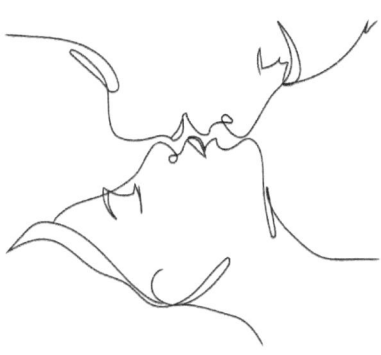

if anything, i am persistent

you say i forced my way in
but i swear you saved me
treading water
waves crashing
and there you were
a helping hand
looking at me like i counted
pulled me to my feet
you say i forced my way in
but i swear you saved me
with kindness
love
a chance

a love letter to those who left me behind

when they didn't have to

here's to the ones who
fix things
they did not break

the piece i didn't know
was missing

we walk through your city
with laugh, stories to tell
and jokes
only you and i know

my cheeks pinch and ache
but from smiling
tears fall
but from gratitude

and if i could show this
to the younger version of myself
i would
i'd play it over and over
and say
look who is waiting for you
it does get better

a love letter to those who left me behind

tied to you

i don't believe in coincidence
when i think of your heart tied to mine
maybe i believe in fate?
as our lives and souls combine
there's no way this is luck
finding you
firm is the line

we got the car to start

amidst the chaos
opinions. insanity.
we crossed paths
what are the odds?
i never believed in luck
but with lady luck i'll dance
if it's her who brought me to you

a love letter to those who left me behind

family

you pulled me in
and snapped my edges into place
like i'd always been here
in this shared space
lazy nights go on and on
pajamas for the entire day
you grabbed my hand
and said you were there to stay
with the love you gave
the time you shared
all of me. no matter what.
no piece spared.

here's to the bones

if you asked my bones
they'd say you've been here all along
from start to finish
you and i belong
they forget the days
the months, the years
when we were strangers
i swear they interfere
they block out the time
when no string was tied
i'm grateful for the lapse
for the bones that decide
we're greater than the time
we ever spent apart
here's to the bones who know
hand in hand and heart to heart

a love letter to those who left me behind

finding our way

when my skin
feels like bricks
heavy to the bone
the thing that keeps me
grounded
is how your love
feels like home

matching spicy brains

i can't remember
how it happened
but here we are
looking at the moon
laughing in my car
one day you were there
open and free
there was room at your table
you made space for me

a love letter to those who left me behind

made sense with each sense

you feel like late summer
humid nights with warm air
windows down, music loud
the wind in my hair
you taste like cotton candy
sugary and sweet
and sound like my favorite song
holding my hand in the front seat

thrilled to write you in

i quite literally stumbled
upon you
it's hard to explain
i'm one of the few
who knows your real name
a long shot, definitely
worth it? without question
things to learn
so many lessons
we figure it out together
i know you're on my team
meeting you was luck
but a literal dream

a love letter to those who left me behind

lady love

you took me in
by the hand
when i needed someone most
the safest of souls
fingers entwined with mine
i knew you meant it
no second guessing
didn't have to hide from your knife
it's like we'd known each other
forever
maybe from another life

a waste

i don't miss you
not really
but i do wish i'd spent my time
elsewhere

a love letter to those who left me behind

tumultuous waters

you thrived on my insecurities
taller with each one you found
kept me right below the surface
       at the mercy of your hands
              i almost drowned

finally
i love you for leaving

it's tough to realize
and understand
but time has made it clear

i love you
for teaching me
how to persevere

even though it was
supposed to be in your favor
your ship to steer

i love you
for leaving me behind
so i could end up here

a love letter to those who left me behind

part five

what really counts...

a love letter to those who left me behind

sharp realizations when i
put pen to paper

this is a love letter
to those who left me behind
i love you for leaving
that's the best you could've done for me
but we both know
that's not why you did it

when it clicks

all this time i searched
turned over every stone
wished on stars
each eyelash i've blown
i made bargains
and promises i couldn't keep
for the love and acceptance of others
i waded waters so deep

i was looking for things i thought i needed
but the jokes on me
because i needed to love myself
corner to corner, soul to bones, fully

a love letter to those who left me behind

this for that

days, weeks, months, and years
that's what it took

to make my way back to myself
the self i bartered and traded
my shine and brightness
dulled and faded

she was worth waiting for

grateful

thank you
for teaching me
how sometimes
it's better to simply
be alone

a love letter to those who left me behind

**you're not missing
you left**

i took down
the missing persons posters
you're not coming back

i feel lighter

this brought her back

this climb isn't for
the faint of heart
challenging, demanding
from the start
but the ridges and cliffs
brought me back
to the girl I almost erased
piece by piece, stack by stack

a love letter to those who left me behind

**draw the line
do not cross**

self-love is
setting the boundary
making the space
saying no
and leaving people
you don't need
because you're not afraid
of being alone

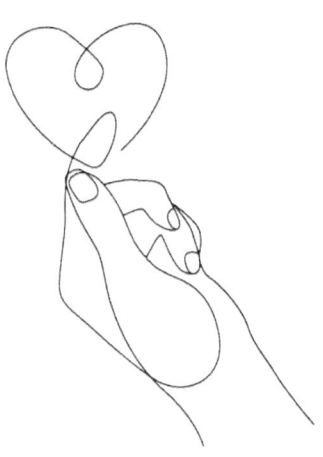

take the space

each thing that wanders
or person who leaves on a new chase
has given you the greatest gift
without knowing it...

they've given you the space
for someone else

a love letter to those who left me behind

too this
too that

love yourself
to make up for
for every
you're too much
you're not enough

strength and time

you can only tread the water
for so long
until you try to swim
and move forward

some days you'll swim with
the current
and others against
but when it feels bleak
remember all the times you treaded water
the muscles you built

you've been through it before
you'll get through it now

a love letter to those who left me behind

me before you

i had to love myself
before i could learn
to truly love someone else

commit to you

it's impossible to show up
for others
if you never show up for
yourself

do it with pride
no guilt
second guessing

show up
because
you love yourself
enough

a love letter to those who left me behind

**healing takes as long
as it takes**

love the intricacies
the quirks and things that
set you apart
be kind to yourself
there's only one
… it had a rough start

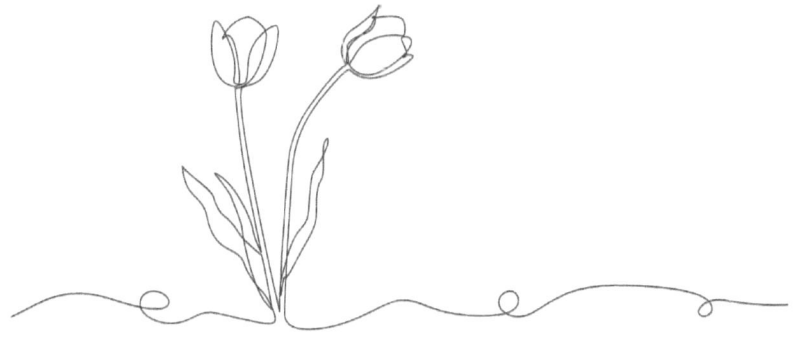

"she's just a lot"

i'm not for everyone
and that's okay

a different version of myself
would crack down the center
at the realization
would cut off the pieces that don't fit
mold the corners
make them soft

i'm not for everyone
and I don't want to be

a love letter to those who left me behind

enablers and introspection

hindsight gets clearer with time
I know now
you
did the best you could
everyone made it seem fine

no one told you that it was wrong
you didn't have the self awareness
this is how
you
tried to belong

in conclusion

i love you for
the lessons you taught
no matter the treacherous dark
my dimming light fought
i love you for
showing "if they want to, they will"
the hardest to grasp
something i remind myself of still
i love you for
taking up an obscene amount of space
because when you left me behind
making room was an issue i didn't face
i love you for
the seasons of doubt and despair
afterwards, blooming never felt so good
even better without you there
i love you for
not loving me, the way i needed
because other people do
you left but i'm the one who succeeded

this is the sign off, the end
my name i'm thrilled to sign

> ***this is a love letter***
> ***to those who left me behind***

a love letter to those who left me behind

acknowledgments

Here's the thing, sharing any sort of creative project is hard. Sharing an entire collection about some of your loneliest seasons? Brutal.

This collection is a lifetime in the making. The only reason this book exists is because I did meet the right people. People who encouraged me to be myself, no matter how loud or opinionated. People who stuck around because they wanted to. People who showed me what it's like to be valued.

Jenna, the person I trusted with the roughest version of this project, your kindness and enthusiasm kept me going, even on the days I didn't feel worthy.

To the people who love me... thank you for sticking with me and letting me love you back.

To my darling husband, Roberto, who continues to help me bloom, I love you.

To anyone who asked me "where my poetry went" or shared my work, you're the reason I didn't abandon this project. And for every person who has picked this up, thank you for making a dream of mine come true... you'll never know what it means to me.

xoxo- Rach

a love letter to those who left me behind

about the author

Rachel LaBerge is the author of *A Love Letter to Those Who Left Me Behind*. When she's not reading or writing, she's probably thinking about donuts, sour candy, or looking for her next hyperfixation. She lives in Michigan with her husband (Roberto), her 2 frenchies (Rafa and Ruby), and cat (Riley).

You can connect with her on Instagram, TikTok, and Threads @rachellabergeauthor (no 'R' name required).

Visit her website at rachellaberge.com.

other books
by Rachel LaBerge

a love letter to those who left me behind

a love letter to those who left me behind

www.ingramcontent.com/pod-product-compliance
Lightning Source LLC
Chambersburg PA
CBHW020415130626
46549CB00006B/2571